I HATE WASHINGTON STATE
303 Reasons Why You Should, Too

Crane Hill
PUBLISHERS
BIRMINGHAM, ALABAMA
1996

I HATE WASHINGTON STATE
303 Reasons Why You Should, Too

by Paul Finebaum

CRANE HILL
PUBLISHERS

Copyright 1996 by Paul Finebaum

All rights reserved
Printed in the United States of America
Published by Crane Hill Publishers
Many thanks to John Carrigan.

Library of Congress Cataloging-in-Publication Data

Finebaum, Paul, 1955-
  I hate Washington State: 303 reasons why you should, too / Paul Finebaum.
    p.   cm.
  ISBN 1-57587-040-1
  1. Washington State University – Football – Miscellanea.   I. Title.
GV958.W38F55   1996
796.332'62'09739--dc20   96-10698
                                                                                        CIP

10   9   8   7   6   5   4   3   2   1

I HATE WASHINGTON STATE

I Hate Washington State Because…

1. President Clinton's famous line "I feel your pain" was initially intended for the Cougars after Washington whipped their behinds in the Apple Cup.

2. Keith Jackson graduated from Washington State's "Whoa Nellie" School of Broadcasting.

3. Mark Rypien has given hope to all WSU quarterbacks—if he can make it in the NFL, anyone can.

4. Of course, Drew Bledsoe has done extremely well. Are we sure he went to WSU?

5. A recent poll revealed the following things would happen if WSU ever made it to the Rose Bowl again: Hell would freeze over.

6. The Seattle Mariners would successfully execute 2 triple plays in 1 game.

7. The WSU Cougars would successfully execute 1 double play.

8. The Cubs would win the World Series.

9. The Seahawks would go to the Super Bowl.

10. Di and Charles would reconcile and remain faithful to one another.

11. Pigs would fly.

12. Richard Simmons would marry Cindy Crawford.

13. Paul Finebaum would write a truly funny book.

14. President Samuel Smith would smile.

15. Does the name Mike Price mean anything to you? Hasn't meant anything to the Cougars since the stiff took over as head football coach.

16. USC coach John Robinson has to pay taxes in Pullman, because he owns Washington State.

17. Kevin Eastman took his team to the NIT last season. Now if he would just take off for good.

18. Streaking is big at WSU—especially 6-game losing streaks in football.

19. So is blowing big leads—like in the 1995 WSU-Washington game.

20. WSU's mascot is named "Butch."

21. WSU used to have a live cougar as the mascot but it smelled better than most of the male students, giving the coeds a difficult decision.

22. Starting in 1998, the Cougar mascot will be replaced by an underclassman dressed as Mercury's sporty-yet-economical auto of the same name.

23. Only WSU seniors are allowed to sit on the Senior Bench, and the Student Vigilante Committee has installed hidden cameras to catch all underclassmen who even just *think* about sitting on the bench.

24. The last live cougar died in 1978–the same year as WSU's football program.

25. Friel Court is a good place to watch a basketball game because there are no NCAA championship banners to block the view.

26. WSU's colors are crimson and gray, which is fitting because after big games the coach's face is crimson and the outlook is gray.

27. The top 10 rejected nicknames for Butch the Cougar are: Lassie.

28. Butcher.

29. Irving.

30. Bubba.

31. Sly.

I HATE WASHINGTON STATE

32. Rin Tin Tin.

33. Lou Zerr.

34. Snuggles.

35. Miss Kitty.

36. Hillary.

37. *Far Side* cartoonist Gary Larson is a WSU graduate. Perhaps that explains the the preponderance of cows in his drawings.

38. WSU's colors are crimson and gray, but after playing UW, they're usually black and blue.

39. A popular saying around the Pac-10 is "A tie is like kissing a WSU girl."

40. What do a hurricane, a tornado, and a Pullman divorce have in common? In every case, somebody's going to lose a trailer.

41. An Academic All-American at WSU is an athlete who can name 2 of his professors.

42. Most followers of WSU football consider the Winnebago to be a luxury car.

43. WSU's most frequent alumni donations are returned diplomas.

44. WSU fans take their kids to McDonald's and actually look for the farm.

45. The only thing worse than a Cougar fan is 2 Cougar fans.

46. When Washington State fans travel to a bowl game, they always take a $20 bill and a pair of underwear–and they rarely change either.

47. Whenever a storm blows over a manure bin near WSU the police have standing orders to shoot all looters.

48. Students take their homework to WSU football games to help keep them awake.

49. Coach Kevin Eastman is fond of saying, "UCLA will be right up at the top again, and so will Stanford. I think it would be a *fun* challenge to be in the mix—to go out every night and have a little pressure on us to perform."

50. Maybe if coach Eastman put a little pressure on himself and his players to perform they *would* be in the mix!

51. Coach Eastman said the things his players do best are run, play unselfishly, and score well.

52. Now he just needs to get them to do those things on the basketball court.

53. WSU students are lobbying to have Dwight Yoakam's hit "A Thousand Miles From Nowhere" introduced as the school's new alma mater.

54. The top 10 reasons why incoming students chose WSU over a technical school are: They didn't want much homework.

55. They wanted more time to date.

56. They wanted more time to drink beer.

57. They figured the teachers would be easier to bribe.

58. There would be little chance of having to deal with heavy machinery.

59. It would be easier to get football tickets.

60. It would be easier to make the basketball team.

61. The lines at the bookstores would be shorter.

62. The competition along the bell curve would be less.

63. "Technical" is a difficult word to spell on job applications; "WSU" is much simpler.

64. WSU professors rarely speak for more than 30 or 40 seconds at a time without becoming flustered and shouting, "Hey, ain't it break time already?"

65. Coach Eastman thinks the mark of a successful team is that the players get better as the year goes on, and he's convinced that his players are getting better and better. It's just too bad every year ends before they get good enough to win.

66. WSU basketball players are not required to visit the library before they graduate. However, they are required to learn to spell it.

67. A WSU grad's idea of hitting the big time is moving to Yakima.

68. The most popular pickup line at WSU is "For a fat girl, you don't sweat much."

69. The most common reply is "Thanks."

70. WSU's graduation ceremony is traditionally followed by a trip to UW to introduce grads to their new bosses.

71. Coach Eastman's brain was rejected by an organ bank.

72. WSU's most popular campus organization is the Hair Club for Men.

73. Due to overwhelming player demand, next year's WSU football uniforms will feature oversize lace collars.

74. WSU students think "safe sex" means closing the barn door.

75. A recent survey showed that 60% of the Washington State football players are making straight As, and most are doing quite well on the rest of the alphabet too.

76. Coach Mike Price utterly confuses his players with his strange tic-tac-toe—they don't understand how there can be so many Xs and Os.

77. President Samuel Smith expects coach Price to go places—and the sooner the better.

78. Athletics director Rick Dickson always has a clear mind—that's because it's not cluttered up with facts.

79. Coach Scott Duncan usually has nothing to say, but that doesn't stop him from saying it.

80. Most people live and learn—sportscaster Bud Nameck just lives.

81. Coach Kevin Eastman is so cheap that he once got mad at his son for paying attention.

82. Adam must have been a Washington State graduate–only a Cougar would take the apple instead of the naked woman.

83. All you have to do to confuse a Cougar basketball player is to put him in a round room and tell him to sit in a corner.

84. When coach Eastman's wife asked him to wash a basement window, it took him all day—he spent the first 6 hours digging the hole to put the ladder in.

85. The NCAA's ban on excessive celebration is due to the embarrassing spectacle of Drew Bledsoe breakdancing after every Cougar first down.

86. Athletics director Rick Dickson recently lost a few pounds—which means that he's not quite as big a fool as he used to be.

87. What do WSU fans call duct tape on the hood of a car? Chrome.

88. When the police stopped sportswriter Bob Sherwin for a traffic violation, he said, "I know I was driving on the wrong side, but the other side was full."

89. Cougar football players think their teammates are pretty.

90. Sportscaster Rick Lukens keeps opening things by mistake–mostly his mouth.

91. A Washington State pre-med student recently completed the world's first successful hernia transplant.

92. When faced with intense pressure to make their weight, WSU wrestlers have been known to have up to 17 yards of small intestine removed.

93. Coach Kevin Eastman's idea of a real treat is to stand in front of the mirror and look at himself.

94. The top 10 excuses given by WSU president Samuel H. Smith for hiring Kevin Eastman as basketball coach are: He had the hots for Eastman's wife.

95. He was drunk.

96. He was high.

97. Eastman begged so much that he couldn't turn him down.

98. He could get the Cougars a great discount on slightly irregular shorts.

99. He was trying to improve academic standards by lowering the quality of the coaches.

100. He lost a bet with the president of UNC-Wilmington.

101. He hates basketball.

102. Eastman was the first applicant he interviewed.

103. It just seemed like the right thing to do at the time.

104. WSU football practice has often been called off for team viewings of very special episodes of *Blossom*.

105. WSU students think they're getting higher education when they have classes on the second floor of a building.

106. What's the last thing a WSU stripper takes off? Her bowling shoes.

107. First prize in a recent radio giveaway was a pair of season tickets for Washington State football. Second prize was 2 pairs.

108. To ensure that his players give 110% every game, coach Mike Price makes them bet on themselves.

109. Washington State alumni think beer tastes better through a straw.

110. Sports broadcaster Dave Grosby should stand up more often to give his brain a rest.

111. WSU's proximity to the Idaho border has prompted a rash of black-market potato smuggling.

112. Until his junior year at WSU, quarterback Mark Rypien dotted the "i" in his name with a heart.

113. After contract disputes with Nike, the basketball team starting playing in used ski boots.

114. The top 10 sportscasters Kevin Eastman hates the most are: Rick Lukens.

115. Dan Kleckner.

116. Carlton Wing.

117. John Carter.

118. Dave Grosby.

119. Bud Nameck.

120. Sonny Sixkiller.

121. Paul Finebaum.

122. Chuck Nelson.

123. The Fabulous Sports Babe.

124. Repeated viewings of *The Bad News Bears* made the Cougars hunger for the "lovable loser" image.

125. Coach Kevin Eastman's written instructions are pinned to each player's uniform with "ouchless" safety pins.

126. Students at UW can eat in world-class restaurants, see major league sports, or visit great museums. However, WSU leaves them in the dust when it comes to cow-tipping.

127. Usually when a Cougar basketball player attempts a 3-pointer, the ball ends up in the rafters.

128. Athletics director Rick Dickson carries a vibrating beeper in his pocket and pages himself all day long.

129. Pullman may not be the end of the world, but you sure can see it from there.

130. Only 23% of all WSU fans have ever used dental floss.

131. President Samuel H. Smith was the role model for Sam I Am in Dr. Seuss's *Green Eggs and Ham.*

132. Cougar football practice is often disrupted for 45 minutes at a time by mirthful linebackers playing "Pull my Finger."

133. Cougar fans think "safe sex" means paying for it with someone else's credit card.

134. The top 10 sportswriters Mike Price hates the most are: John Wiley.

I HATE WASHINGTON STATE

135. Larry Henry.

136. Bob Condotta.

137. Ron Newberry.

138. Bud Withers.

139. Blaine Newnham.

140. Steve Bergum.

141. Laurence Miedema.

142. Chadd Cripe.

143. Bob Sherwin.

144. Mike Price's revolutionary halftime strategy allows his players to nap for 20 minutes so they'll be "April fresh" for the second half.

145. The best thing about going to school in Pullman is that it's more than 30 minutes away from the nearest Domino's, so the pizza is always free.

146. The lack of crowd noise at Friel Court during games makes it an ideal place for quiet reflection.

147. The science department at WSU has solar panels aimed at the moon.

148. Caning must be legal in Los Angeles because the Cougars get beaten every time they play there.

149. The best form of birth control at WSU is nudity.

150. Mike Price's best joke is his record against USC.

151. Many of the Cougar players were shocked when someone explained that Dr. Scholl's wasn't the team doctor.

152. WSU's economics department offers a course in "Counterfeiting the Xerox Way."

153. Paul Finebaum's column is required reading for all Cougar players. Audiotapes are provided for those who can't read.

154. When freshman basketball players were asked if they knew who Jack Friel was, the top 10 responses were: The lead singer for the Eagles.

155. The Michigan suicide doctor.

156. Some rich dude they named the basketball arena after.

157. A character actor on *Beverly Hills 90210*.

158. The inventor of the Flowbee.

159. Bob Dole's running mate.

I HATE WASHINGTON STATE

160. A friend of Brian Blades.

161. Governor of Washington.

162. Joan Rivers's new husband.

163. The cop in the O. J. trial.

164. A po'boy is anyone who sits through an entire Cougar basketball game.

165. President Samuel Smith is a legend in his own mind.

166. The bestselling bumper sticker in the WSU bookstore is "Wait Till Next Year."

167. President Samuel Smith often contradicts himself—and he's usually right.

168. Coach Kevin Eastman is always on edge during games due to the constant bouncing noise.

169. Fourth-quarter huddles often involve the Cougar quarterback saying, "No, I haven't got any ideas either, but I would like to take this opportunity to pass out some Binaca."

170. The Cougar weight room features equipment by La-Z-Boy.

171. You can always spot a WSU bride because she's wearing white overalls.

172. Drew Bledsoe could have been a Rhodes scholar at WSU if it weren't for his grades.

173. Whenever the Cougars lose a basketball game, the players say, "Hey, you try playing when you know you're missing MUST SEE TV!"

174. A dope ring is 5 WSU players standing in a circle.

175. At least once a year the guy in the Cougar costume loses it and mauls someone in the crowd.

176. The Cougar football team's defense often avoids physical contact with the other team in the second half on the grounds that "those guys are all messy and sweaty."

177. Most WSU students have ambivalent feelings about deodorant.

178. Coach Mike Price was so moved by a documentary he saw about hunger in Central America that he had his wife bake 12 batches of cookies and send them to Cleveland.

179. The top 10 uses for *The Daily Evergreen* are: Lining birdcages.

180. Killing flies.

181. Always good in a pinch in the event the Charmin is finished before you are.

182. Great for starting a bonfire.

183. On a boring night, the editorials are usually good for a laugh.

184. Good to help clean mud off shoes.

185. Effective in hiding the face of a typically ugly WSU coed.

186. If you pretend the letter "W" is Waldo, it makes for a pretty easy game of "Where's Waldo."

187. It's a great forum for third-grade writing.

188. There aren't many more decent things to do with the rag.

189. The WSU athletic department attempted to boost ticket sales for Cougar football games with the slogan "Come on down, they might do something cute."

190. When Kevin Eastman asked his doctor how to cure his insomnia, his doctor replied, "Try listening to yourself talk."

191. An attractive woman on WSU's campus is obviously a visitor.

192. WSU students believe that drinking Diet Coke will help them lose weight and get high at the same time.

193. The dean of WSU's law school once said, "The worst thing about our jury trial system is that you leave your fate in the hands of 12 people too stupid to get out of jury duty."

194. WSU grads make great fast-food restaurant employees.

195. Cougar athletes like to play David & Goliath with their jockstraps.

196. WSU students think that *The X-Files* is a TV porno show.

197. Quite often coach Kevin Eastman gets his playbooks mixed up with his coloring books.

198. Most WSU students think that low-fat milk comes from skinny cows.

199. The top 10 reasons students visit Holland Library are: It's a great place to pick up dates.

200. If your roommate is studying, the upper stacks are a good place to make out.

201. It has the best Hardy Boys collection in the Pacific Northwest.

202. It's the only library in Washington to have Paul Finebaum's entire *I Hate* collection.

I HATE WASHINGTON STATE

203. It has the uncut film version of *Deep Throat.*

204. It also has the uncut version of *Louie, Louie.*

205. It has samples of Shawn Kemp's new fragrance.

206. It's the only place on campus with clean restrooms.

207. It's a good place to smoke pot.

208. It has back copies of *The Daily Evergreen* if you really need a good laugh.

209. Kevin Eastman's biggest win at WSU was overcoming the flu.

210. The longest rush from scrimmage last year by a WSU running back was to the sidelines for an "ouchless" Band-Aid.

211. The WSU biology department never has to buy lab rats—they just look under the seats at Friel Court.

212. WSU has installed slot machines in the locker rooms—for quarterback use only.

213. The school's flagship station KIRO is often confused with a favorite sandwich of the football team.

214. Before registration WSU students are required to be up-to-date on all of their immunizations—including rabies.

215. Cougar basketball players enjoy disrupting games by sucking the air out of the ball to get a quick buzz.

216. Cougar football players spend 20 minutes at a time staring at orange juice cans that say "concentrate."

217. WSU students think "panty raid" is roach spray for underwear.

218. WSU cheerleaders have income tax figures and they should be arrested for not filling out their forms.

219. A number of Cougar football players have their positions listed on the roster as "drawback."

220. Cougar basketball players think that the ruler of a country is 12 inches tall.

221. President Samuel Smith has gotten so old that his thoughts have drifted from passion to pension.

222. The top 10 pickup lines on the WSU campus are: You don't smell bad for a WSU coed.

223. Hey sweet thing, do you wanna see my new tractor?

224. Do you happen to know Keith Jackson? He's a friend of mine and I can't seem to find him.

225. Do you have the time? My daddy is president of Boeing and I need to pick him up at the airport.

226. You look familiar–did I meet you at Bill Gates's party last week?

227. You look familiar–did you have a part in *Sleepless in Seattle* too?

228. My last name is Nordstrom and I can't seem to find my father's store.

229. You weren't one of those girls who filed suit against Bob Packwood, were you?

230. You look familiar—were you an intern on the design team for Windows 95 too?

231. Nice buns.

232. The food is so bad at WSU's cafeteria that they have Mylanta on tap.

233. When a reporter pointed out that Mike Price was actually WSU's third choice for head football coach, Price replied, "That's okay–I was my wife's fourth choice."

234. To cut out the irritating squeaking sound, the Cougar basketball players have started playing in Birkenstocks.

235. The Cougars unofficial fight song is "Send in the Clowns."

236. Cougar players frequently get out of practice because of "breaking a fingernail."

237. A strong wind would knock over WSU's defensive line.

238. The Cougars think defense is something that needs painting every few years.

239. WSU's student body is constantly under fire from the NAACP for being "too white."

240. Incoming WSU freshmen think SEX is a Greek organization on campus.

241. WSU's football program peaks in July.

242. Coach Mike Price's top 10 reasons why going to a Washington State football game is better than having sex are: Nobody has to perform well.

243. There's usually less noise.

244. You don't have to worry about how you smell.

245. You don't have to act like you're enjoying it.

246. You don't have whisper.

247. It lasts longer.

248. Most Washington State men get more for their money at a football game.

249. You won't have to see your wife for 4 hours or so.

250. There's no reason to fake a headache since the game will give you one.

251. There's little chance of procreation.

252. Mike Price is the Chevy Nova of college football coaches.

253. The lack of desire on the WSU football team is perhaps best exemplified by the fact that most special team players leave during the third quarter in order to beat the traffic.

254. You can say one thing about Mike Price—he is as graceless in defeat as he in victory.

255. Classes at WSU are often confused with 4-H club meetings.

256. Keith Jackson graduated from WSU magna cum loudest.

257. The best thing Dick Vitale can say about the Cougar basketball team is "These guys have shown a lot of improvement in the area of dental hygiene, baby!"

258. Coach Mike Price doesn't think holding should be a penalty if the other guy is hurting inside.

259. Most WSU fans think defense is something to keep the cows in.

260. Most WSU students think South America is where Alabama is located.

261. Coach Kevin Eastman said that sportswriter Paul Finebaum reminded him of Moses. Finebaum thought it was a compliment until Eastman added, "Yeah, every time he opens his mouth the bull rushes."

262. One WSU professor is working on a book entitled *Water and Ice: The Hidden Connection.*

263. President Samuel H. Smith promotes his university by saying, "Unlike *some* schools I could name, WSU's professors won't be skipping classes anytime soon to accept any of those fancy Nobel Prizes."

264. There is something to be said for coach Eastman, and he is usually saying it.

265. The top 10 pastimes of WSU football players are: Picking fights with coeds.

266. Picking fights with small children.

267. Watching tapes of the Jerky Boys.

268. Trying to correctly guess the last time the WSU team won an important game.

269. Taking a field trip to Microsoft to see a real winner in action.

270. Picking fights with stray dogs.

271. Picking their nose.

272. Picking their friends' noses.

273. Passing drills.

274. Passing gas.

275. Coach Mike Price has only 2 faults: everything he does and everything he says.

276. WSU's recruiting efforts suffered a terrible blow when it was revealed that the football team dines on nothing but stale Chee-tos and Fresca.

277. Like the leaves, WSU's football team falls every autumn.

278. It shouldn't surprise anyone to learn that WSU is a land-grant university.

279. Kevin Eastman can say less in more time than anyone in the world.

280. Mike Price secretly wants to coach at UW.

281. Most WSU students think O. J. Simpson is Bart's father.

282. Despite WSU's desperate petitioning, the Pac-10 isn't going to be the first conference to convert to the Nerf football.

283. Coach Mike Price started at the bottom and stayed there.

284. Misguided environmentalists on WSU's campus are often seen carving "Save the Spotted Owl" into the trunks of 100-year-old redwoods.

285. The top 10 career goals of WSU basketball players are: Stay out of prison.

286. Be a gas station attendant.

287. Be a bowling alley attendant.

288. Be the fry man at McDonald's.

289. Be the Frosty man at Wendy's.

290. Be a Domino's delivery man.

291. Be a Fuller brush salesman.

292. Be Mike Tyson's sparring partner.

293. Be a college basketball player.

294. Be a college graduate.

295. Bob Packwood is often seen lurking around the WSU campus attempting to "poll the electorate."

296. Mike Price once said, "My problem is I'm now coaching at one of the schools I'd want to play."

297. WSU's definition of an oxymoron: A good season in football.

298. WSU's second definition of an oxymoron: A good season in basketball.

299. I don't about oxymoron, but moron describes Rick Dickson.

300. Wes Werner serves as the WSU sports information director—talk about an impossible job.

301. WSU fans have a love-hate relationship with coach John Robinson of USC–they'd love him to retire because they hate losing to him every year.

302. Jackie Sherrill and Dennis Erickson both coached at WSU–what else needs to be said about the school's integrity?

303. The biggest seller at the campus bookstore this year will be *I Hate Paul Finebaum* by Tommy Charles.